Half Full

Meditations on Hope, Optimism, and the Things That Matter

Conari Press

Mina Parker

PHOTOGRAPHS BY DANIEL TALBOTT

Half Full

Meditations on Hope, Optimism, and the Things That Matter

Mina Parker

PHOTOGRAPHS BY DANIEL TALBOTT

INTRODUCTION BY JAN JOHNSON DRANTELL

First published in 2006 by Conari Press,
an imprint of Red Wheel/Weiser, LLC
With offices at:
500 Third Street, Suite 230
San Francisco, CA 94107
www.redwheelweiser.com

Library of Congress Cataloging-in-Publication Data

Parker, Mina.
Half full: meditations on hope, optimism, and things that really
matter / Mina Parker; photographs by Daniel Talbott; introduction
by Jan Johnson Drantell.
p. cm.

Includes bibliographical references and index.

ISBN-10: 1-57324-293-4 (alk. paper)
ISBN-13: 978-1-57324-293-6

1. Optimism. 2. Conduct of life. I. Title.

BJ1477.P37 2006

170'.44—dc22

2006006356

Typeset in Linotype Avenir and Bembo

Printed in China
MD

10 9 8 7 6 5 4 3 2

Introduction

A simple glass of water can cure a lot of ills. I have a friend who says if you wait until you're thirsty to drink water, it's kind of too late. Your body is depleted. When I saw this book, I had the idea that the book itself is kind of like a glass of water. Its beautiful images, inspiring quotes, and insightful, sometimes piquant, meditative essays might satisfy a metaphorical thirst.

I think this book is an invitation to sit for a minute. At the beginning of the day, at the end, or somewhere in the middle. To put your feet up. To browse *Half Full*. To let yourself go where the words and pictures take you.

The best thing this book can do is help us see our own lives through varied perspectives. Is the glass half empty or half full? From what angle are we looking? What are we looking for? This lovely book helps us see. Whether you're taking a moment to count the blessings that add up to a glass more full than empty, or filling up and replenishing when that glass is getting low, I hope the photos and words here bring a bit of respite, an "aha" or two, maybe a smile, just when you need it.

— Jan Johnson Drantell, San Francisco, 2006

one

Half Full

Half Full

Glasses are everywhere. Kitchens, restaurants, bars, and stores. And, of course, in our mind's eye. We use the real ones to mix up lemonade, have some milk with our cookies, even whip up an impromptu flower arrangement. And those metaphorical glasses can get us down if we feel they're half empty, or they can inspire and energize us when we see them half full. Maybe some are more full than others. But the trick is that, half full or half empty, it's the same glass.

Half full. It's like a movie musical. Times are grand, life is sweet, and that crazy man is singing and dancing his way through a rainstorm. When we're looking at the world with our rose-colored glasses all shined up, and the glass is half full and getting fuller, just think of the possibilities. We're in a place to love more, give more, do more.

C'mon in and explore your inner optimist. It's a cliché. It's an attitude. It's a way of life. Keeping ourselves optimistic isn't really all that much work. We've just got to make the effort, keep trying, and choose to see the good that's all around us every day, in little ways and big ones.

Gloomy gray to opaque black—hipper, smarter, more edgy, interesting, avant-garde folks look at the world that way. So it must be better or smarter or artier. But who says bleak equals artistic?

Maybe looking at the world as if things are better than they are might sometimes be a way of actually making them better than they are. Just sometimes, not all the time.

Truth be told, the best windowpane to view the world through is a clear one. Not colored by our prejudices toward pessimism or optimism. But it seems as if that's not always possible, so I say, take the rose over the gray, whenever you can.

Rosiness is not a worse windowpane than gloomy gray when viewing the world.

—**Grace Paley**

What do you want to look at through rose-colored glasses today?

I am like this about plants and kids. I can get down about work, about my relationships with friends and family, about myself. But I love to water the plants. I love to pick off the dead leaves, check the soil, linger over coming blooms. I'll put hours into the things, and never notice the time passing. (My mother kills plants handily, but has this kind of boundless enthusiasm for reading and writing.)

Same with kids. I can spend days playing, thinking of new ways to learn, or fun, silly things to do, with no notion of wasted time or stress. Unlike many other things, this doesn't make me feel taken advantage of or resentful of the amount of work it takes. How can I transfer this unending energy into other things in my life? It's worth a try.

The most noteworthy thing about gardeners is that they are always optimistic, always enterprising, and never satisfied. They always look forward to doing something better than they have ever done before.

—Vita Sackville-West

Transplant a cutting of optimism from one task to another.

Here it is, in a nutshell. We all have a choice. See the world how you want. There are tons of opportunities and heaps of difficulties in everyone's life. This is an unchangeable and real given. So here's where your wonderful perspective comes in. See a possibility—a new job path, a blooming relationship—and what happens? Do you immediately immerse yourself in thoughts of what could go wrong? Do you rein in your desires because you're afraid of getting hurt?

Now look at the difficulties—face them head-on. What do you see? Toil and frustration without compensation? Or can you see steps, even painful ones, on the path to a goal? Things worth accomplishing are difficult, and the course of true love never did run smooth. No news here. So why not take another look and see the opportunities hiding in the cracks of every difficulty, and acknowledge the difficulties inherent in any opportunity?

A pessimist sees the difficulty in every opportunity; an optimist sees the opportunity in every difficulty.

—Winston Churchill

Look for an opportunity in a difficulty that's been dogging you.

Tightrope walkers forget how high they are, and musicians lose themselves in the piece while the fingering does itself. Seem impossible? Well, that's the power of the positive.

Mental blocks are more paralyzing than physical ones. More importantly, mental force is more empowering than physical force. We know this is true. If it weren't, lighter, weaker boxers would never be able to beat stronger, more skilled ones. And yet it happens all the time.

Your own negativity, or the negativity of those around you, can very easily sink down beneath your feathers and into your skin, so waterproof that duck's back. Negativity can sap you of your energy, strength, and imagination. So flip it, and look at the bright side. Or if that fails, stuff your fingers in your ears and sing loudly.

That's my gift. I let that negativity roll off me like water off a duck's back. If it's not positive, I didn't hear it. If you can overcome that, fights are easy.

—George Foreman

Put positive thinking to work for you, as you work to master something complex and difficult.

I have one surefire way to send myself into a downward spiral. And I don't think I'm unique in this at all. One word—comparison. Two words—odious comparisons. As soon as I start comparing myself to (a) others around me, (b) who or what I imagine I should be as a mother, a wife, an artist, (c) who I think my friends and family think I am, or (d) all of the above, I can get to feeling like dog dirt in about sixty seconds flat.

We get a ton of help in this culture, weighing in on the "what we should be" side. Commercials, for instance—we should, or at least could, be thinner, younger (looking), stronger, with whiter teeth and toilet bowls. Self-help books, doting mothers who only want the best for us, hit-it-big-time college roommates—all of them can make us feel as if we should be, or at least be doing, something else.

Antidote for above: Live an examined life. This is not a one-minute, one-time cure. I won't get it in prime time. And I won't get it from anyone else. I will get it only if I pay attention to my life and to who I am and who I want to be, thoughtfully, maybe with a dollop of humor, at least once every day.

A man should look for what is, and not for what he thinks should be.

—Albert Einstein

When you're brushing your teeth, who do you see in the mirror?

Sometimes I catch myself being a selective optimist. When I'm giving (pouring, in this case), I'm filling up the glass and it's always half full. Those on the receiving end, I think, ought to feel very lucky to have this wonderful half-full product of my love and caring.

But when I'm on the receiving end (drinking, in this case), I sometimes feel cheated. Sure, I'm getting something from a situation or a person, but it's really not all the way. It's half empty, and I'm starting to resent it.

Maybe it's time I pulled a switcheroo. When I'm giving, I'd do better to remind myself I could always do more, always top it off and fill 'er up. And when I'm getting, it might be better to appreciate it and see the fullness of the gifts.

Is the glass half full, or half empty? It depends on whether you're pouring, or drinking.

—Bill Cosby

Bring your optimism to the fore, and watch as resentment transforms into gratitude.

So many times people say they need to get away. They need a tropical vacation. They need a new house. They need a change, maybe a new job. Vacations can be good. So can new houses. And new jobs. We all know that "different for the sake of different" is not necessarily better or more enlightening, but sometimes we forget it.

I grew up in a city where the weather changes from flat-out rain to sunny and back again in minutes. There's an old adage that if you don't like the weather there, you should just wait a minute.

Looking at something with new eyes might mean waiting "a minute." By morning that insurmountable obstacle might become an opportunity no longer in disguise. So take a minute. Sit in a different corner of the room, and take a new look.

The real voyage of discovery consists not in seeking new landscapes, but in having new eyes.

—Marcel Proust

When's the last time you looked at your own eyes?

I knew a family with two dogs—they were both mixed breeds from the pound, though one seemed most likely a border collie type, and the other was more of a bulldog mix. The family was well off and had an apartment in the city and a weekend home in the country. All week, the collie mix would mope around the house, alternating between being lackluster/bored and hyper/obnoxious. The bulldog mix, however, was in heaven, lolling on the couch and slobbering all over anyone who sat there. Then, on the weekend, the tables were turned. The collie was in her element in the country, running and running outside, while the bulldog was clearly put out to have to hang out in the elements (of any kind) and move around so much while the family played.

Dogs get a certain amount of their disposition from their breeding, and they get along best in an environment that suits them. And we're like that too, but we have a choice about our outlook in a given circumstance. We all know people who bounce from place to place, job to job, or partner to partner in search of happiness, when maybe all they need is a change of attitude.

The greatest part of our happiness depends on our dispositions, not our circumstances.

—Martha Washington

Make the connection between mind-set and mood, in good times and tough ones.

Funny, I know an optimist who thinks everyone is as positive as she is, and loves them for it. Sounds more fun.

There really doesn't seem to be a final word on the nature/nurture debate about how we get to be who we are. But I think it's a pretty sure bet that how we look at other people stems some from how we were taught to as children. And, yes, it's a good idea to teach children not to talk to strangers. But maybe it's also a good idea to spend some time figuring out how to make a stranger a friend. And to discern between dangerous strangers and everyone else who is not out to get us.

A pessimist thinks everybody is as nasty as himself, and hates them for it.
—**George Bernard Shaw**

What does it feel like to smile at someone I don't know?

Wake up, stretch,
and look at all that
sweet grass!

My mother keeps a Rumi poem on her fridge about the cow who lives alone on a deserted island. Each morning, she wakes to a beautiful day and a hill covered with fresh, sweet grass. She spends her day happily munching away, and by dusk she has eaten every last blade and grown plump and satisfied. But as the sun sets, she thinks, "What will I do tomorrow now that I've eaten all the grass? I'm going to starve!" As the night passes, her fear at the thought of her starvation gains momentum with each breath until she literally wastes away to skin and bones by sunrise. Then, in the dawn light, she sees that the hill is fully replenished with sweet green grass (maybe even more, she thinks, than the day before). Again she eats, growing happy and full by the end of the day. But again in the night she worries about tomorrow and wastes away to nothing in her terror.

Even if you don't enjoy the same plenty today that you had yesterday, in fact *especially* if you don't, won't you be better off if you don't spend your night wasting away your energy, your spirit, your drive?

Did you know that the main definition of a weed is any plant growing where it is not wanted? There are places where water lilies grow wild, clogging whole ponds. Wild roses can take over and grow into massive, unruly bushes. Turns out, a weed is just in how you look at it.

The best gardens are planned carefully, tended each step of the way, but with an eye open for happy accidents. My family moved into a new house when I was eleven. The backyard was a mess, overgrown. My father and I managed to carve out a place for a box where we planted bulbs—daffodils and tulips. We cut back the rosebush and trimmed and seeded the lawn. Then, during the rainy season, we got a surprise. Out of the somewhat sandy, very wet ground sprouted bunches and bunches of calla lilies. Totally unplanned and unplanted. Those weeds filled vase after vase in our house until spring.

No garden is without its weeds.

—Thomas Fuller

Always leave room for happy accidents.

Today is a great day. I've had a full night of sleep and I woke up to bright sun shining in the window. I've got family and friends whom I love and share my life with. I've got new things to learn and enough health, energy, and drive to accomplish so much of what I'd like to do. There are endless great books to read, oceans of wonderful people to know, tons of good food to cook and eat, time to walk, go to museums, listen to music, dance.

My life doesn't have to be perfect to be fantastic. Tomorrow doesn't have to worry me unless I let it. Yesterday is done and gone, whatever happened, good or bad. And today is a gift that's new every morning.

I am not afraid of tomorrow, for I have seen yesterday and I love today.

—William Allen White

Today, let the good stuff stick to you like honey.

What a nice place to live. Emily Dickinson wasn't Little Mary Sunshine by any means. She was a woman who looked at her world with a realistic and wry eye. So I think we can safely assume that Possibility is a real place and we might all dwell in it, if we give ourselves half a chance to settle in there.

As long as we're alive, when *isn't* there possibility? I suppose there's just as much possibility that things will get worse as that things will get better. But that's not how I choose to read this snippet. I choose to see that there is always positive possibility. Until we are dead there's the possibility of life.

I dwell in Possibility—

—Emily Dickinson

What's possible in your life?

A day at the beach. A happy holiday at home. A perfect visit with your parents. A lovely meal with friends. And, then, seemingly just as it started, it's over. "Oh, well," we say, "all good things come to an end."

Yes, they do. But so do most bad things. And what if we applied the same amount of energy to telling ourselves that all bad things come to an end as we do to knowing in our bones that all good things do?

The spat with a friend, the painful trip to the dentist, the frustration of not being able to finish a project may not seem to be over in the blink of an eye. But at least we'll have reminded ourselves that they will be over.

Life is sweet. Everything bad comes to an end.

—**Alfonsina Storni**

Sometimes I can even choose the end of a bad thing in my sweet life.

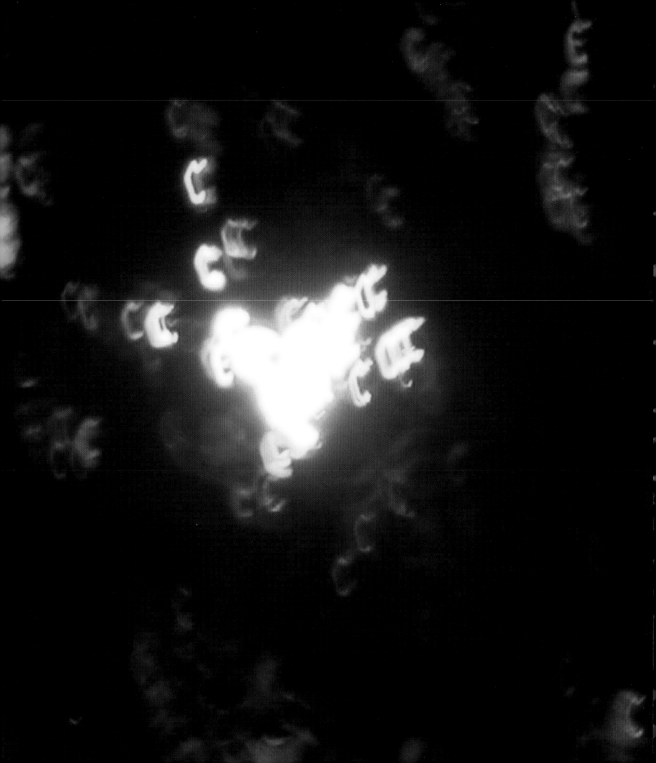

The history we learned in school is the history of war—of conquest, conflict, empire. And the tyrants and murderers are the protagonists—marching, winning, oppressing. Then, usually in a sentence or two, maybe a whole paragraph, we get the story of their demise. The end of the terror or hatred is confined almost to a footnote. Maybe the textbook editors don't think it's as compelling when truth and love win.

Perseverance is the key. The bad guys can't win forever. A new door always opens, a new path begins, and darkness always recedes. Our job is to maintain hope and stamina to create change in ourselves, our lives, and the world. But also to be fortified by Gandhi's thought and know that the wait is worth it. Always.

Remember that all through history the way of truth and love has always won. There have been tyrants and murderers and for a time they seem invincible but, in the end, they always fall—think of it, ALWAYS.

—Mahatma Gandhi

Even the darkest, most invincible powers will be vanquished, if by nothing else than time.

Potential is a funny thing. In one way, it's just an idea—not real yet—just a maybe. Yet it can inspire you or stymie you, just the same. But the truth is that potential can never be taken away from you. There is always a possibility, always a maybe.

You don't know what the future holds, but instead of letting it worry you, get stirred up by what is possible. I've just recently started putting more biographies on my reading list. People I admire in my field, or people with lives far from my own in time, space, and circumstance. When I'm struggling, it's a great comfort to read through the trials that someone before me lived through. And when I'm floating, the stories of others' achievements are an exciting inspiration.

Everyone has inside him a piece of good news. The good news is that you don't know how great you can be! How much you can love! What you can accomplish! And what your potential is!

—Anne Frank

You have the potential, now get busy!

> *I feel no need for any other faith than my faith in the kindness of human beings.*
>
> —**Pearl S. Buck**

An actor friend who has struggled for years and years doing nonpaying gigs and keeping up a grueling day job opened a card this Christmas. It was from someone on the board of one of the theaters where he had been working for the past couple of years, toiling away, receiving great reviews, and really getting noticed. In the card the board member wrote how important this actor was to the theater community in the area, and how much he appreciated the work he was doing and wanted to support it as much as possible. And he included a check for $15,000. The money has literally changed my friend's life, allowing him to cut down on his day job and focus more on his real passion.

People are amazing. Often when you least expect it, people are willing to go out of their way to lend encouragement, support, cash, manpower, love. So even when I can't muster up faith in the universe, or the justice system, or religion, I can remember to have faith in those around me.

Make a donation, send an action e-mail, do something for someone in need and restore your faith in humanity.

She's so full of herself—that's a cliché we use to say that someone thinks too much of herself. (Usually when we're feeling inadequate, threatened, or inclined to less-than-useful comparisons of ourselves to said person.)

But maybe it's not a bad thing to be full of myself. Maybe it's better if my glass is half full—and getting more full—maybe even in danger of overflowing. And maybe instead of worrying about when the juice is going to start leaking out, when the good stuff is going to go away, maybe I could just appreciate myself. And express my gratitude to the friends and family who help bolster my self-esteem.

And find a way to pass it on—because if I'm full of myself, there's no reason you shouldn't be, too.

An individual's self-concept is the core of his personality. It affects every aspect of human behavior: the ability to learn, the capacity to grow and change. A strong, positive self-image is the best possible preparation for success in life.

—Dr. Joyce Brothers

Let yourself feel full of yourself.

two

Half Empty

Half Empty

Ever know one of those super-resilient grandma types? The ones who, when asked how they're doing, reply, "It could be worse . . . I'm not dead yet!" and then let out a huge cackle? Or one of those inveterate grouches who will moan and complain all day long, but then you catch a quick wink and a wry smile? Or just someone who can spin a fantastic, funny yarn out of their most embarrassing or trying moments? These are the positive pessimists. The secret optimists. They know how to look at a glass half empty and see it for what it is—a task to be done, something better than nothing, or the makings of a good joke.

There are times. Nothing is going right, or so it seems. Things are going downhill fast, and your attitude is crummy. Or maybe even things are going just fine, but you still can't quite feel great. That's when you have to call in the reserves. When you have to tap into your stores of humor, of willpower, of perseverance. These are the moments for creative optimism. The glass is half empty anyway, so drink it, or pour ice in there, or dump it over someone's head. In short, shake things up, put your nose to the grindstone, and get yourself out of the hole.

Dark times are difficult. There are times when whatever I know about staying in the moment, let alone loving it, is just a bunch of meaningless blather. Even the little things can get me down. There is no way I'm going to love the moment when I've just slammed my knee on the footboard of my bed. (And I do this kind of often.) I do love the bed, but I don't love the moment, and I wish I had (a) a bigger bedroom, or (b) the same bed with a narrower footboard, or (c) both. But I don't.

The bed came the way it is. The room came the size it is, and it's not so small, by city standards. And it's the most comfy bed I've ever had in my life. And my husband's grandma made us a present of the most beautiful comforter in the world. And so that's a little flower I can find in the moment I bumped my knee. And, if I pay attention, maybe I can love other times when darker moments hit.

How long has it been since you've given yourself a flower?

Guess what? You're going to fail at something. There are going to be moments, hours, days, when you step back and think, "Forget this, it's not doing me any good." Guess what? Maybe it's time to get a little more comfortable not being right all the time, not feeling great. Maybe it's time to take yourself a little less seriously—maybe even (gasp!) laugh at your failures.

Next time you're feeling pessimistic, go ahead . . . indulge it to the max. Seriously, go whole hog. My husband is really good at this. I'll complain about money, or work, or something, and he'll say, "You know, you're right. We should really give up. We're penniless, our friends all hate us, we have ugly clothes and furniture, and really nothing is ever going to go right again."

And, even through clenched teeth, I have to smile.

I was going to buy a copy of The Power of Positive Thinking, and then I thought: What the hell good would that do?

—**Ronnie Shakes**

Exaggerate your troubles to the point of ridiculousness. Laugh them away.

In the middle of the doughnut is the hole. If you eat the hole instead of the doughnut, you lose weight. That's an opportunity. In the middle of a sleepless night there comes a thought. If you write it down, you may have the seed for a new business plan. That's an opportunity.

An opportunity is not an instant solution. An opportunity is not something that makes you thin or creates a successful business overnight. An opportunity is a little light on the path that you still have to walk. An opportunity is a cart to carry the load. The load's as heavy as it ever was, but it sure seems a lot lighter when it's not on your back. And once you get going, the downhill stretch is going to be that much easier because the cart will roll on its own.

In the middle of difficulty lies opportunity.

—Albert Einstein

What's in the middle of your difficulty?

If you want the peanut, you gotta put up with the shell. As I see it, there are two ways of getting things you want. You can wait for them to appear, as in the case of rainbows. Because nobody can make a rainbow. Or you can do the work to get it, as in removing the shell from the peanut.

And, really, neither one is intrinsically better than the other. The key is recognizing what you want and whether it's a "go out and work hard for it" thing or whether it's a "wait until the circumstances are right and it can come into your life" kind of thing. Because good things come by both modes, no doubt about it.

The way I see it, if you want the rainbow, you gotta put up with the rain.

—Dolly Parton

When's the last time you waited, happily and expectantly, for a rainbow?

So the glass spilled, and there's metaphorical grape juice all over the white rug. Or you got dumped by your boyfriend the same week that your boss decided she could get along better without you—oh, and in the meantime, your cat killed the neighbor's canary, and your car popped out of gear, rolled down the hill, and plowed into some nice old lady's prize rosebush, so now she's coming after you with her high-priced attorney in tow. Well, slapstick is what that is.

And not any fun while we're going through it. But if, when the you-know-what hits the fan like this, you can close your eyes for a minute and simply say, "Someday maybe I'll see the humor in all this," well, then, someday you'll probably see the humor in all this. And maybe that day will be soon.

My mother wanted us to understand that the tragedies of your life one day have the potential to become comic stories the next.

—**Nora Ephron**

May you laugh
tomorrow.
(Or today.)

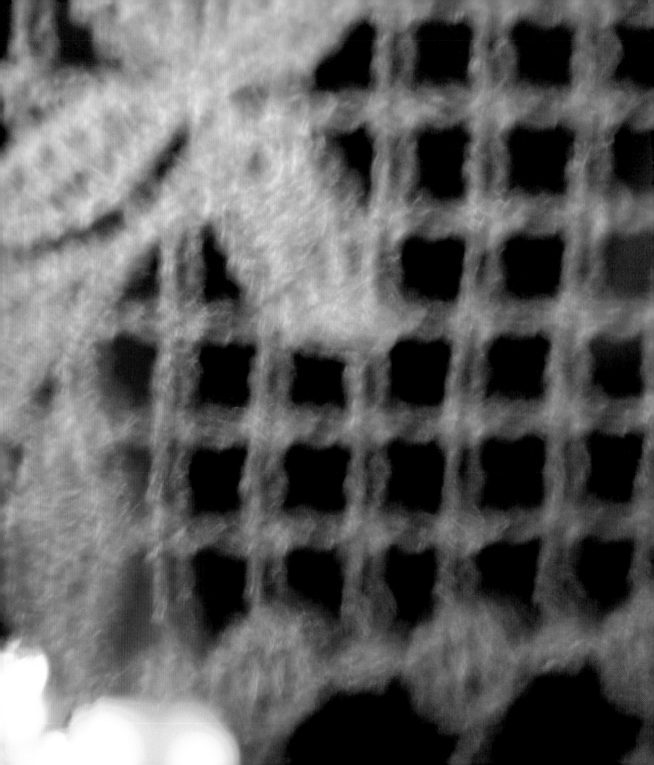

I never knew the great-grandmother I'm named after. But there are stories. She was a great cook, a seamstress, and one of those women who made do, especially during the Depression, when she was raising four children and her husband didn't have a job. She made sailors' caps, admirals' hats, paper boats, and who knows what all else by folding newspaper. Oatmeal cartons and cardboard boxes turned into fancy painted castles. And when my grandmother and her sister needed new dresses for a special occasion, they all went downtown, tried on the fanciest gowns. Then, off to the fabric counter, and soon the girls had the dresses of their dreams.

Lots of families have these stories of how mom and dad or grandpa and grandma made do when times were tough. I suppose they're romanticized, maybe exaggerated. We don't see the whole picture through these stories.

Still. They're inspiring. And every once in a while, I find myself hungry for lemon pie.

When life hands you lemons, make a pie.

—**My great-grandma**

Tell yourself the story of one setback that turned into something good.

Maybe the glass is not half empty, or half full, but totally, completely bone-dry empty. Really. Huh, is this a kind of optimism I see creeping in? Unless somebody kicks the glass over or turns it upside down, it's bound to get a few drops of rain, at the very least.

Expectation can be a great disappointer or a great motivator. Walker knows this, and she betrays her own optimism when she brings surprise into the picture. If you empty your mind and your heart of expectations, I guarantee you will be surprised. Count on it. Expect it, even.

Expect nothing. Live frugally on surprise.

—Alice Walker

Keep your mind clear and your eyes open, and allow the world to surprise you today.

The 1910s, the Great War; the '20s and '30s, the Great Depression; the '40s, World War II; the '50s, the Cold War; the '60s and '70s, Vietnam and cultural chaos; the '80s, Reaganomics; the '90s, the first Gulf War; the 2000s, the bursting of the stock bubble and more war in the Middle East. Whew. It sure hasn't gotten much better since Emerson was around.

Or has it? Even though it inspired a litany of horrors, I think this quote actually reflects a positive mind. Don't fret about the times being bad and the money being in short supply. It's never been any different, and it probably never will be. And wonderful things filled the past century as much as awful things did. And many more wonderful things are on the way.

Can anybody remember when the times were not hard and money not scarce?

—Ralph Waldo Emerson

Don't bother brooding about how bad it is—the bad may always hang around, but the good will pop up too, surprising you all the way.

Our senses don't deceive us: our judgment does.

—Johann Wolfgang von Goethe

Practice really seeing whatever it is you're looking at.

Sometimes what I see is a glass half full of the good things life has to offer—laughter, companionship, fun, resources. And I'm fine until I get to thinking and thinking and judging that what I think I see is not enough—I'm going to run out soon. My friends are leaving town. My bank account is running low. I'm tired and at the end of my rope. I judge my glass half empty.

Of course, the sad thing is that by judging my glass half empty I pretty much guarantee that it is. And then I tend not to see things for what they probably are. I don't hear the concern in a friend's voice when she calls. And I chafe against her sound advice because I think she's judging me for getting into a jam in the first place. And then maybe I snap at her. And she snaps back. And we both hang up mad. And she's thinking she won't soon call again, and there it is. My glass is half empty and getting emptier.

If I had paid attention, instead, to the words my ears were hearing, well, then, things might have turned out differently.

I am one of those people who like to do counting exercises. I find myself counting the number of times I stir the pancake batter. Or the number of steps I'm taking down the block. Or ticking off on my fingers while I complain about each of the number of things that went wrong at work today.

When I catch myself doing that—and I try to—I then try to remember that I can count positive things as well. Counting positive things doesn't mean I have to ignore the very real negatives in the world and in my life. But it does give me a different perspective. It can calm me down, and it can bolster me to gird my loins and take on those negative dragons 'til at least some of them are breathing flowers instead of fire.

People deal too much with the negative, with what is wrong. . . . Why not try and see positive things, to just touch those things and make them bloom?

—Thich Nhat Hanh

Can you count to ten in good things you see around you?

Someone told me a story about Michael Jordan—in high school, his team lost the championship, and the coach was about to go home that evening when he heard someone in the gym. He went in to find Michael practicing alone, after losing the biggest game of the year earlier that day. The coach was astounded. When he asked what Michael was doing there, Michael told him he was practicing for next season. No surprise he's considered maybe the greatest to ever play the game.

He knows that your thinking, whether before a big shot or during a life-changing moment, can mean everything. To think of the consequence of missing is to let in the "what-ifs" that pull your focus from the task at hand. Better to plow your energy and heart into a bigger goal and remember that one shot doesn't make or break a career.

I never looked at the consequences of missing a big shot . . . when you think about the consequences you think of a negative result.

—Michael Jordan

When you've got a tough task, think of its place in the larger picture.

> *There is no cure for birth and death save to enjoy the interval.*
>
> **—George Santayana**

F asten your seat belts, ladies and gentlemen. And welcome to life on planet Earth. Babies generally don't need to be reminded to enjoy the interval. When they are happy, babies are totally, absolutely, 110% enjoying the interval. And babies tend to spread it around. The next time you see a baby in a store or restaurant, check it out. People smile and nod, say hello, talk to the parents. Babies make nodding acquaintances out of strangers. Just the thought of a giggling baby can bring a smile to most of us.

Some of the best flirtations I've ever seen are between babies and people old enough to be their great-grandparents—people who are just beginning to enjoy the interval and people who've had a lot of practice doing so. I like to think they both get something from each other.

There's no time like the present to begin enjoying the cure.

Chicken Little. Remember her? "The sky is falling, the sky is falling!" And then the world is ending. But, of course, the sky didn't fall.

I don't think pessimism knows any age boundaries. I talk to friends my age who are pessimistic about the future of the world because the people our parents' age, who are running the world, are making a mess of it. I talk to friends my parents' age who think the world is going to pot for any number of reasons—mostly depending on whether they stand left or right of center on the political spectrum, which seems to have nothing to do with where they stand on the optimism spectrum.

So, it doesn't cost anything to, at least once in a while, pretend that things are going to turn out okay, whatever the world's current troubles are. And, if they don't, well, as the man said, you'll at least have been cheerful for a while.

While there is a chance of the world getting through its troubles, I hold that a reasonable man has to behave as though he were sure of it. If at the end your cheerfulness is not justified, at any rate you will have been cheerful.

—H. G. Wells

Be reasonable—
imagine
everything's going
to work out.

Now. Now. Now. Pin your hopes on this moment. But don't make the mistake of forgetting what has been or discounting the possibilities of what may be—those things exist in the now too, in memories, histories, plans, and dreams. All of it, combined in this second now, and this next one, and the next, is *perfect*. Just as you, with all your ticks, mistakes, talents, insecurities, and successes, are *perfect*, and (this may seem like a paradox, but I swear it's true) *getting better*.

We spend so much of the day lost in making plans or trolling in our minds through the recent or ancient past. It's so easy to forget to immerse ourselves in the here and now. Really, we can't be anywhere else but here and now, but our brains will try like hell to convince us otherwise.

[There] will never be any more perfection than there is now.

—Walt Whitman

Shut off your brain for a while and revel in the perfection of each moment as it comes.

We humans are pretty great at losing perspective. The middle of winter, and we know it's not going to be this dark forever, not even for another couple of months, but it can really get us down. Then summer comes and all we want is a cool breeze and a dark night by the fire with a book.

In college we had to write a paper defining "poetry," and the professor made the point that any definition must make a fence around a word. It must tell us what goes inside the fence and what belongs outside. In other words, the only way to know what something *is* is to also know what it is *not*.

The glass can only be half full if it is also half empty. And a glass brimming over all the time is just making a big puddle—you'll probably forget how great the plenty is if you're always stuck mopping up the extra.

There are as many nights as days, and the one is just as long as the other in the year's course. Even a happy life cannot be without a measure of darkness, and the word "happy" would lose its meaning if it were not balanced by sadness.

—Carl Jung

Give yourself a definition of optimism with room for the bad stuff too.

A friend pointed out to me recently that she thought I did some of the best work in my career at a moment when I had the most going on—the most deadlines to meet, the most stress, having to deal with too many people wanting too many things done right away.

Don't make a habit of surrounding yourself with stress, but when those moments come along—and, of course, they will—think of them as a blessing. Sometimes, in the eye of the storm, you can find a strength and a focus you never knew you had. We all read stories about incredible untapped human potential, mental and physical, and scientists tell us we use only a small percentage of our brain capacity in our lifetimes. Let the worst times work for you—watch as the extraneous nonsense falls away and the tasks before you become clear.

In times of great stress or adversity, it's always best to keep busy, to plow your anger and your energy into something positive.

—Lee Iacocca

Let the energy you put into worry and procrastination flow into what needs to be done, and do it.

You'd rather take a cloudy day over no rain for a year, a crummy cup of coffee over lost lunch money, any abundance over any deficit, a bit of something over a ton of zip.

Positive thinking might take a bit of practice. Sometimes, when I fall into thinking that I have nothing, the world is pretty much against me, and all I'm having is bad luck, I challenge myself to spend a day, or even an hour—or just ten minutes, if things are really dire—thinking about something positive. I don't have enough money to take my husband out to a four-star dinner on his birthday. I do have enough money for groceries to make something we both love to eat.

Sometimes a little positive can help offset even the biggest negative.

Positive anything is better than negative nothing.

—Elbert Hubbard

Positives come in different shapes and sizes.

What is going to serve the people I love, my work, the world? What is going to be more useful? We may think our fear and negativity are products of logical, intelligent thinking. But what if we really evaluate how our thinking affects our life in every way? What then?

Some groups call it "stinkin' thinkin'," that negative thought that seems right there on the tip of our brains and tongues. I can't . . . because it will be too hard. It won't work. I don't have time. Someone else should do it. Somebody else will mess it up. Besides, no one can solve all the world's problems.

True. And, as Winston Churchill said, it's more useful to be an optimist. That way you might solve some of the world's—or at least your own—problems.

For myself I am an optimist—it does not seem to be much use being anything else.

—Winston Churchill

What if I asked myself the worst thing that could happen, and it wasn't so bad?

Imagine. Galileo. Marie Curie. Einstein. Martin Luther King Jr. Imagine them lolling around feeling sorry for themselves, sure that even though they had some good ideas, the world would never accept them, they would be ridiculed and humiliated, and change would never happen. Wait— they were laughed at, scorned, and worse. And they were still optimistic enough to plow ahead. And they all changed human history.

Pessimism is petty. It may feel deep, it may feel right, but here's a good test: What great achievement by a pessimist do we remember? I can't think of one. We can only achieve great things if we believe it's possible and if we can silence, at least for a while, the whiny little nobody who'd like us to stay put and not accomplish our dreams.

No pessimist ever discovered the secrets of the stars, or sailed to an uncharted land, or opened a new heaven to the human spirit.

—Helen Keller

Chart the path to your next achievement, great or small.

three

Filling Up

Filling Up

Replenish. That's a nice word. Fill up again, and when you're running on empty, fill up again. And again. Renew, refresh, and revitalize. But how?

We could all use a day at the spa, a long walk, a vacation. And yes, those are great ways to get some distance and some perspective on our lives. Do these things for yourself whenever you can, and really let yourself enjoy them.

But you can't give your outlook a massage and facial, so how can you fill up those reserves?

I try to take an indirect approach. When I was a sulky teenager and would complain to my father about a headache (real or imagined), he would say, "Wait right there while I get a hammer," and then he would mime bashing my toes with it so I would "forget" all about my headache. It was an awful joke, but sometimes did the trick.

You can't forget about your fears or troubles by thinking them away. In fact, the more you think, the larger they tend to loom. Our energy flags. We get tired. Hungry. And the world doesn't look like such a friendly place. Problems are bigger. Our glasses are less full. So take your mind off the half empty, and put it on some task. Have faith in yourself and your abilities. Putting your energy outside of yourself and into the world is a great way to fill up your glass on the sly. Then look back and savor your accomplishments, and enjoy the fullness you've earned.

Always. You know this. You notice them at the corner store, at the supermarket, even in the coldest winter. Even in the middle of the city, where an unexpected window box of geraniums catches your eye. All that red. Flowers are flowers are flowers, and no botanist can tell a kid that those bright yellow flowers are weeds.

Dandelions all over the backyard. Remember when you used to rub them on your chin to see if it turned the skin yellow?

There are always flowers for those who want to see them.

—Henri Matisse

Find yourself a
flower today.

I think what Santayana meant to say is, "Get over your bad self." Or, once we get outside ourselves, stop worrying about every hangnail and when we might get hit by whatever it is we're afraid of getting hit by—cancer, bankruptcy, a truck—we're going to have an easier time navigating our everyday lives.

Not only that, we'll no longer be our small, midgy selves, with our petty concerns foremost. When we're not living in fear, we tend to give more back to the world. We see those glasses as half full, and we help fill them up—our own and others.

Let a man once overcome his selfish terror at his own finitude, and his finitude is, in one sense, overcome.

—George Santayana

What am I afraid to say I'm afraid of?

When I was a child, I'd sit at breakfast and stare at the back of the cereal box. I wasn't reading the words, and I wasn't really thinking about anything. And sometimes things would come to me, ideas for projects or a specific memory, or just an overall feeling of feeling good. I guess in my adulthood I'd name that feeling "well-being."

I could be the winner of the spelling bee or the lead in the school play or a famous explorer. I could see myself doing whatever. It seemed possible, and I had no sense of obstruction or jealousy because someone else might be a better speller or have more time to explore.

That childhood daydreaming is difficult for adults, or at least for me, to recapture. I know what it's not—it's not about not liking my life, about wishing I were someone else, somewhere else, doing something else. So if I can leave all that behind, I can—and do—recapture that feeling of well-being. All's right with the world. And I can see myself doing whatever it is that it comes into my mind to do, without thinking of all the obstacles.

> *Optimist: Day-dreamer more elegantly spelled.*
>
> **—Mark Twain**

The next time you're tempted to be a daydreamer— do it!

Woulda, coulda, shoulda—that triplet of despair and helplessness. Why is it that some children with incredible potential, even those labeled geniuses or prodigies, are often stymied when they become adults? Could it be that the expectation of their success and the mental energy it takes to sustain the ideal of their own perfection overwhelm the physical energy and stamina they need to really make use of their talent and intelligence? True learning and growth require failure and the ability to change and build on existing skills. The energy we put into woulda, coulda, and shoulda saps us of the power we need to make use of what we have.

The question for each man to settle is not what he would do if he had means, time, influence, and educational advantages, but what he will do with the things he has.

—Hamilton Wright Mabie

Experiment with eliminating the conditional. Don't talk about what you should or would do, but what you will or won't do.

J ust do it," says the slogan that sells shoes. Get it done. Write a list. You can make it as long as you want (don't bother getting overwhelmed, you're not going to be able to finish it all today). Then put stars next to three things to accomplish today. Things you can do, that you don't have to wait on someone else for. And finish them. Then cross them off the list in the darkest black marker you have. And if you still have some time and energy, tackle a few more.

The short run counts and the long run matters—and the only way you know that for sure is to do. Then you can see the results, reap the rewards, enjoy the outcomes.

An idealist believes the short run doesn't count. A cynic believes the long run doesn't matter. A realist believes that what is done or left undone in the short run determines the long run.

—Sydney J. Harris

Indulge the idealist and the cynic at the same time—by just doing it.

Remember that list you just made? And all the doing you've been doing? Time to throw yourself a curve ball. Time to take up your big black marker and cross a couple of things off *without doing them*. Or, if that makes your eyebrow twitch, try moving them to another list, and putting that list in an envelope marked "Open three months from now on (date)." Maybe a few things on that perpetual to-do list in your head are dead weight. Thankless tasks that won't give you any enjoyment or even a satisfying sense of accomplishment. Do you really need to feel guilty that you haven't put the pictures from last year's vacation (or for that matter, every vacation you've ever taken) into an album? That should be a nice, easy weight to take off your shoulders.

> *Besides the noble art of getting things done, there is the noble art of leaving things undone. The wisdom of life consists in the elimination of non-essentials.*
>
> —Lin Yutang

Do the essentials, both practical and soul-fulfilling, but let the rest go.

I've been thinking about how babies learn to do things. My mom tells about the first time I rolled over. She put me down on my back in front of a friend's Christmas tree because I loved the lights. She put me just out of reach of the crib scene, with a shepherd that caught my eye. I wanted that shepherd.

I reached and I reached and I reached, and then I rolled. And I grabbed the shepherd and laughed out loud, or at least that's how my mom remembers it. And then, life being life, and crèche scenes being made out of breakable china, she had to take it away from me. But I still knew how to roll over to reach something I wanted. I used my frustration, and I didn't even know I was doing it.

So, even if we don't consciously remember doing it, we've used our frustration, all of us. That's how babies learn. And it's why books and grandmas tell you to let a baby be frustrated once in a while. Encourage, but don't solve all the baby's problems.

You've done it before and you can do it now. See the positive possibilities. Redirect the substantial energy of your frustration and turn it into positive, effective, unstoppable determination.

—Ralph Marston

Let yourself reach through the frustration.

Some things have to be done. For instance, I have to organize our receipts if I'm going to file our taxes. Whether it's been a prosperous year or not. Whether it's going to take me all day, or whether my new filing system works and I'm going to find everything our tax guy needs and put it together in just an hour or two of concentrated effort.

I know this. Yet, I think about how hard it's going to be. I imagine that I won't be able to find a statement I need, and I'll spend days looking for it. Or I imagine how quickly it's going to go and what I'll do with the rest of the Sunday afternoon I've set aside to do it.

All of that imagining—good and bad—is kind of wasted effort. Because, sooner or later, warm water or cold, I'm just going to have to do whatever it is I'm going to have to do. I can't change the fact that I have to do it. And sometimes the way to do it is not to pay too much attention to the voice in my head, whether that voice is saying, "this is going to be hard" or "this is going to be simple."

It doesn't matter if the water is cold or warm if you're going to have to wade through it anyway.

—Pierre Teilhard de Chardin

When's the last time I made something harder than it had to be?

You may not even realize how many negative thoughts you let creep in. Sometimes they even hide behind positive ones. When's the last time you gave someone a compliment ("What a great dress!") and felt the tug of competitive self-doubt? Challenge yourself to look at the world and seek out the positive. Acknowledge any lurking, nasty underbelly—know it's there and call it what it is—jealousy, or anger, or fear. Then let it go.

Meditate for a bit and come up with three satisfying memories, three positive thoughts and/or goals for today, and three totally out-there wild hopes for the future. Let yourself smile. Then pick one thing you are not looking forward to doing today and find a way to think about it in the most positive light possible. Instead of picturing the pile of laundry, remember how good it feels to slip into clean, crisp sheets at night. And let yourself smile.

Once you replace negative thoughts with positive ones, you'll start having positive results.

—**Willie Nelson**

If you can rephrase your inner monologue, your outlook and your outer world are going to get better.

Create your own scenarios.

J oin me in a little exercise in seeing what you're looking for. Imagine that it's morning, you're running late, you set your full coffee mug down to pick up your keys, but they're not there. They must be lost, you think. You'll never find them, you think. You dig through a week's worth of newspaper and mail. No keys. You check your watch. You're going to be late. You search high and low for ten minutes, getting all the more frustrated. You come back to your coffee, but when you reach for it, it slips out of your hand. You grab some paper towels, bend to wipe up the spill, stand up fast, hit your head, knock yourself out.

Same scenario, different process. You reach for the keys. They're not there. You take a breath. You think about where you last saw them, what coat you were wearing last night. No keys, but a twenty-dollar bill. That's good. You don't have to stop at the bank for lunch money. You think again. Remember the phone ringing just as you came home, find the keys next to the phone. Remember that your friend called to ask you to dinner. So you get in the car, with the keys, and there's no traffic, and you're not late, and you've remembered that you get to have dinner with a dear friend tonight.

I met a woman who had a terrible phobia of clowns—sounds silly, but it's apparently somewhat common. She had kids, and she felt awful not being able to take them to the circus, and even worried about passing on the fear to them. She knew that clowns posed no real danger to her, but even thinking about one made her break out in a cold sweat. Seeing them made her panic and cry and have to take herself out of the situation. She went to a specialist, who took her through a series of exercises to expose her to her fear in small, manageable ways. They started by looking at a drawing of a clown, then a photo. Over weeks, she worked up in this way to her biggest challenge: being in a room with a live clown. There were others in the room with her, and the clown was told not to look at her or interact with her at all. When he entered, she shrieked but she didn't run and was able to calm herself down by breathing, hiding her face, wringing her hands. She only lasted a few minutes, but when she got outside, she gushed to her doctor. Looking back on the experience, she could relax, smile, laugh at herself, and realize how proud of herself she could be. She had stopped her cycle of fear and taken control of it through simple, concrete actions.

You gain strength, courage and confidence by every experience in which you really stop to look fear in the face. . . . You must do the thing you think you cannot do.

—**Eleanor Roosevelt**

Find some small way to tackle a fear you have, large or small.

F ear can rule our lives, change how we act, restrict our most important relationships. If we let it. Not only do we have the choice to face our fears—we must, in fact, as Eleanor Roosevelt says, do the things we think we cannot do. And the best way to overcome fear is to motivate yourself to move beyond it. Once you decide to tackle your fears, you can start to take action.

If you fear snakes, watch part of a nature documentary. We all fear death, but it might ease some anxiety to have a will in order, or to write a plan for your own remembrance. Take action in the face of fear, and then relish looking back at your own growth and preparing to meet the next challenge.

Decide that you want it more than you are afraid of it.

—Bill Cosby

It's always possible to choose to overcome your fear.

Sometimes it seems that the universe has it in for you. One annoyance piles on another, misfortune looms, and though you feel like you are putting your all into it, you just can't crack a problem. The thing we forget in these moments is that true achievement takes true risk. And we, being reasonable people, spend a lot of our time and energy avoiding risk. So it's natural that the moment right before a breakthrough of any kind is the toughest to live through. If you're starting an exercise regimen, it's the moment you think your body might actually shut down and collapse, even though rational thinking tells you this won't happen.

Take heart from the thought that if things are really rough, and you feel as if you just can't do it any more, you're probably on the verge of something great, or at least something new and different.

When you get into a tight place and everything goes against you, till it seems as though you could not hold on a minute longer, never give up then, for that is just the place and time that the tide will turn.

—Harriet Beecher Stowe

When you feel like you can't take it any more, take a breath and hold on.

Years ago I met a man who told this story: He was an infantryman in World War II, captured by the Germans toward the end of the war. They marched their prisoners across country, trying to avoid the Allied troops. There was no food. One day they stopped outside a farm-yard. As John tells the story, he made eye contact with one of the German farmworkers, who slipped him a potato. That man could have been shot on the spot. That was the day John decided to become a priest.

Generosity and optimism go hand in hand. To be generous under extreme circumstances can be acting "as if." As if I have enough money to give away—and if I give it away, there will be more. It can also be an act of hope—if I give away my last piece of bread, there is hope that humanity is still, well, human, no matter what we do.

Courage is not the absence of fear, but rather the judgment that something else is more important than fear.

—Ambrose Redmoon

Practice a random optimistic act of kindness today.

> One does not know—
> cannot know—the
> best that is in one.
>
> —**Friedrich Nietzsche**

You are special. No, wait—don't put down the book. Think about it first for a minute. It's absolutely true. Never before and never again will your particular mix of talent, dreams, ambition, and imagination exist on this planet. What you will accomplish in this lifetime is beyond your wildest dreams. You can plan, study, pray, but you will never know exactly who and where you will be ten years from now, even six months from now.

This is a wonderful gift. It means that inside you, at this moment, there are billions of potentialities. The best of you is in there, and you get the rewarding task of figuring out how to bring it to the surface whenever possible. It also means that you've never achieved the best of the best—that would mean pinpointing "the best," which is, of course, impossible. So keep on going, because the best is yet to come.

Dig down and try to imagine the best in you. Then know that it's even better.

My grandfather was fond of clichés. And he wasn't the most optimistic person I've met in my life, either. One of his favorites was "I must have gotten up on the wrong side of the bed today."

Now I like to think about the days I get up on the right side of the bed. These are the days when things are going right. I wake up in a good mood, for no reason I can discern, and I get everything on my to-do list done by noon. Sometimes things fall into place, people call me back, and projects I've been trying to get going for months happen as if by magic. I feel so good I let myself start something new.

I'm going to remember these days when I wake up feeling like I can't do anything, and even if I do something it won't make any difference to anyone anyway. That's a promise to myself.

Optimism is the faith that leads to achievement. Nothing can be done without hope and confidence.

—Helen Keller

Give yourself the gift of optimism, one day at a time.

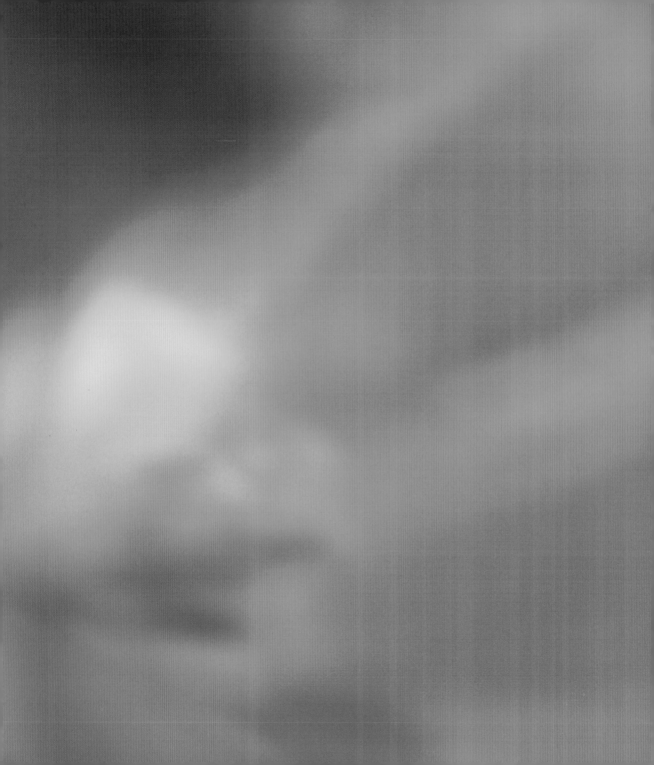

A playwright friend of mine writes award-winning plays full of tortured characters and dark plots with a wonderful, twisted sensibility. And he's twisted, in his own wonderful way—but in a different way than you might imagine. He has no money, lives with his cantankerous mother and her angry cat, has a less than perfect love life, and a perpetual sinus infection. I always expect him to be contrary, down on himself and the people around him, and generally gloomy. But he's a true realist-optimist. In his words, he's a darn Pollyanna. And he can laugh and laugh at the crazy life he leads and the insane world we live in. And he is, at his core, truly hopeful—for himself, for his writing, for the friends he loves, and even for the psychic health of the world. He gives some of the best pep talks of anyone I know. Some may find him impossible, unrealistic, unbelievable, annoying—but I can't imagine a better way he could live his life.

A positive attitude may not solve all your problems, but it will annoy enough people to make it worth the effort.

—Herm Albright

Be relentlessly positive—and savor getting on the nerves of the worst curmudgeon you know.

You know how you feel when you're in a rut? Try noticing the verbs you use, both in conversation and in your inner monologue. Too much dreading? Schlepping? Gossiping? Not enough meditating? Dreaming? Giving? It happens to all of us, every day, in small ways and big ones. And maybe this Swedish wisdom can help by reminding us to tip the balance in favor of some of the verbs that fill our cups instead of emptying them. If you aren't sure you can stop whining cold turkey, you can still surely do less of it.

Fear less, hope more; eat less, chew more; whine less, breathe more; talk less, say more; love more, and all good things will be yours.

—Swedish proverb

Replace your verbs, change your actions, and see how you feel.

To every thing, turn, turn, turn." Change is the only constant. The more things change, the more they stay the same. Did I mention that clichés are clichés because they're true? How did Ovid know that matter is indestructible? Did someone tell him each of us, thousands of years later, would be breathing the same air as he did? Literally, scientists say it's true. We are breathing the air molecules of the ancients. And that's not the only thing that's the same. We have their genes, their wisdom.

It's obvious that everything changes all the time—a simple fact of life. But the secret corollary to transformation is that nothing dies. Things must change, and do, and rebirth is an absolute money-back guarantee.

All things change; nothing perishes.

—Ovid

Renew and refresh, and go with the flow of the changes in your life.

four

Drinking In

Drinking In

There are flowers everywhere. Reasons to celebrate. Things going right. When our glass is half full, we get to reap some wonderful rewards. Feeling successful, letting in light and laughter. Taking the time to imagine, and finding the courage to fulfill the promise of our dreams. The glass is sitting right there, on the windowsill. There's sunlight streaming through it. The breeze is warm, and the drink is cool. It's half full. I pick it up and drink from it. I take it in. My smile radiates to the corners of the room. Even the dog notices. Sated.

Think of what it's like watching a baby who's sound asleep. Seeing that pure release. A quick grimace or a half smile, and you know she's dreaming. And then it's gone, back to the depths. In our deepest souls we have all the courage, imagination, joy, and inspiration we need. Bring the half-full glass to your lips, and feel a touch of hope down to your toes.

In some places it's harder to feel it than in others, but in any place with a cold, dark, winter, you can't mistake it. The smell always does it for me. The air filling your lungs is wetter and softer.

I hate winter. Cold burns at my skin and throat. I feel confined indoors and uncomfortable outside. The dark gnaws away my energy, and the bare trees and ground depress me. So spring is an unbelievable gift. I think it's forsythia, that wild yellow bush, that blooms first. And sometimes I'll even see a hyacinth bulb come up through the snow. Hah! Take that, winter!

And once in a while I'll come across a person like this. Someone who, just by the very fact of their being, seems to be a happy combatant against the blues, the doubts, the anger, the pettiness. This person can light up your afternoon, or if you're lucky, your life. And we could all stand to become a little softer, a little greener, and a little closer to blooming.

An optimist is the human personification of spring.

—Susan J. Bissonette

Bring the spring into your life today with flowers, a smile, and the idea of rebirth.

S pread it around, because what goes around comes around. If you want to laugh, the best thing to do is to try to make somebody else laugh. Try it. Dare you. Maybe on an elevator, or in an airplane, or even church. Kids are easiest. Start with them.

Smiles are even more contagious. Sure, that's been said and said—on 3,176,242 television commercials, and in 15,142,175 magazine articles, and in approximately seven billion self-help books in thirty-five galaxies. (Are we cheerful yet?)

Harmless cheerfulness—not at the expense of others. And not at great cost to ourselves. We're all enriched when we laugh, smile, and gently tease ourselves and others.

I feel an earnest and humble desire, and shall till I die, to increase the stock of harmless cheerfulness.

—Charles Dickens

Who can I cause to smile today?

It's wonderful to get what you want. Sometimes I'll crave something for days at a time—French onion soup, or a berry tart from this bakery I love. And if I can't get it right away, that's okay. Elongating the wanting makes me even more excited to dig in.

But this is even better. Ever get something you didn't know you wanted? And then when you got it, you couldn't imagine life without it? The best gift givers have this down to a science—picking out something you don't already have, or didn't even know about, and fulfilling a desire that you didn't even know you harbored.

A pair of mad green gloves you wear every day in winter. A CD you'd never heard before but that somehow feels familiar. A day of sailing on open water.

By all means, get what you want. And while you're at it, go ahead and get ready to want what you get, whatever it may be.

Success is getting what you want; happiness is wanting what you get.

—**Ingrid Bergman**

Take up the challenge to find a gift for someone that they wouldn't get for themselves, but will probably love.

Ah! Cheerfulness, the bottomless glass of refreshing water. Take a deep drink, use some up, and, presto, it's full again. It's almost impossible to intentionally deplete our reserves of cheerfulness.

When I was little, at the end of the day, when my folks picked me up from day care, my mom would sometimes, teasingly, ask me if I had any kisses left for her. The way she tells it, I always did. I guess little kids instinctively know that you never run out of some things.

So how do we forget that cheerfulness is more contagious than the common cold? That we never run out of kisses? And that, in fact, the more we give away, the more we have. Really, could anything be simpler?

So of cheerfulness, or a good temper, the more it is spent, the more it remains.

—Ralph Waldo Emerson

Give some good cheer away today. How full is your glass?

Great news. I don't have to be normal. Thank god. It happens when I watch too much TV (I should probably just throw it out the window, but I haven't gotten that far yet). I'm sick, on the couch, and I just gaze and absorb it all. Big mistake. Suddenly, I'm measuring up every facet of my life with impossible—and inane—yardsticks. I'm way ahead of those fools on *The Montel Williams Show*, but I sure wasn't infamous and rich at twenty-three, so life is probably over for me.

We all know that the perfect 1950s Cleaver family "normal" is not for everyone (or almost anyone). But the seeming variety surrounding us today must be a little more inclusive, right? Wrong. It's the same old stories about the same old relationships, recycled with new hairdos and more "edginess." And really, our idea of normal doesn't bear much resemblance to actual reality. It can't, because "normal" changes from person to person and moment to moment. So hallelujah—I don't have to worry about measuring up to the crud on TV or even up to the people around me.

Normal is in the eyes of the beholder.

—Whoopi Goldberg

We're always going to have a different "normal," and thank the heavens for that.

It's a temptation, maybe *the* temptation, of our consumer culture. We get the car, the job, the clothes to go with it all. The house, the furniture, the flat-screen TV—and then we want the next thing and the next and the next. It's what makes our economy, and to a certain extent our culture, work.

Uh-oh. Now you feel guilty. I'm not telling you to stop shopping, return to the land, and weave your own toilet paper. But what happens if we slow down the moment between desire and gratification? All marketing is geared to close that distance between wanting and having—so much so, we hardly get a chance to want anything anymore. And wanting, like hoping and trying, can be great. By slowing down, we can savor what we already have. We can remember how we dreamed of having what we have now—a job, a partner, some peace and quiet. And that can make having feel just as good as wanting, if not better.

Do not spoil what you have by desiring what you have not; remember that what you now have was once among the things you only hoped for.

—Epicurus

Remember how much you've wanted all that is wonderful right now.

It makes so much sense on paper, as a philosophy, even as pretty simple physics. When you walk into a dark room at night, you don't turn off the lights to make it light. You turn them on.

What's the alternative to acting like the playground bully when we get punched in the nose by said bully? What's the alternative to dropping bombs that kill innocent civilians when we are bombed? What's the alternative to spreading rumors and gossip?

This is a meditation without answers, because each situation and each person is different. Dr. King's words can fall on our open ears in different ways at different times.

Darkness cannot drive out darkness; only light can do that. Hate cannot drive out hate; only love can do that.

—Martin Luther King Jr.

Find a way to let some light into your life today.

Be careful what you water your dreams with. Water them with worry and fear and you will produce weeds that choke the life from your dream. Water them with optimism and solutions and you will cultivate success. Always be on the lookout for ways to turn a problem into an opportunity for success. Always be on the lookout for ways to nurture your dream.

—Lao Tzu

Remember that old saying: It doesn't cost anything to dream.

Y ou look out for your kids, your parents, your bank account. You problem solve; you make it work. It's not always perfect—but then, what is? Did you forget to look out for your dreams? Did you forget to plant and tend your deepest desires? It might be hard work, but the harvest might surprise you.

And, then again, once you get into the habit of nurturing your dreams, they might grow faster, bigger, and more brightly than you ever dreamed possible.

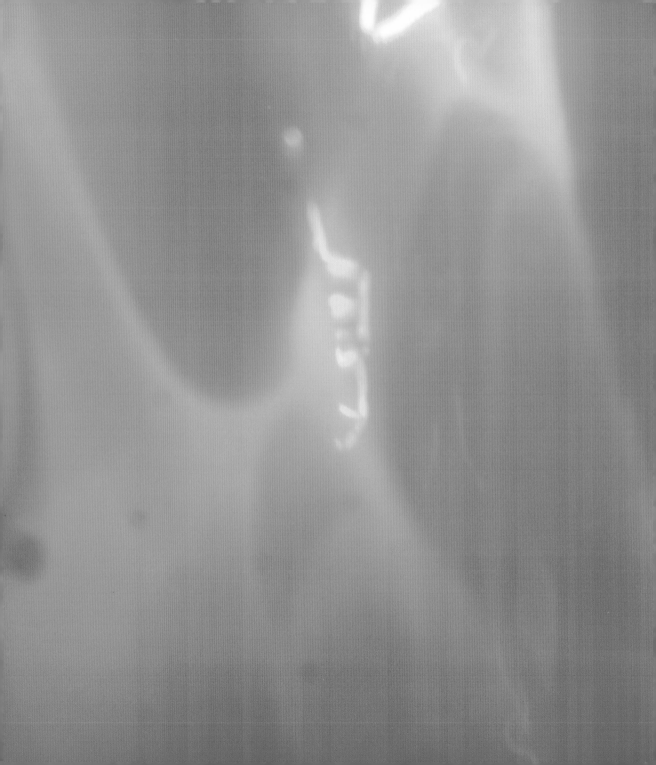

The world is full of inspirational stories about people who believed in things and made them happen, against all odds. People who started schools, who built businesses, who won independence for their people—all they have in common is that they believed in a thing. And we know in our bones that's what made it happen.

I don't think this means that everything will happen just as you think it will. This is belief on a different level—belief that goes inside out and head to toe. I'm not even sure our conscious mind has much to do with it. What you *can* do is try to remove the mental blocks we all put in the way of our own success. Put aside the fears and insecurities that keep you from giving over fully to your belief, and go for it.

The thing always happens that you really believe in; and the belief in a thing makes it happen.

—Frank Lloyd Wright

Bring belief without limitation into your life.

I read the story of a man who had been diagnosed with prostate cancer. He's in remission now, doing wonderfully well, but he talked about something his wife pointed out to him. He was in the midst of a horrible, draining course of treatment and was able to stay very optimistic. He spoke to his wife often about beating his cancer, and felt sure his positive attitude would help.

One day, after his doctors gave him the news that the treatment was not going as well as they'd hoped and they were going to try a new tactic, the man seemed particularly upbeat. Later that evening, his wife pointed out very gently that she knew he might be less positive than he was pretending to be. He was pumping himself up with his own fear, not with actual hope. It was a huge relief to him that she saw both his weakness and his strength, and a great boon to him to understand that being courageous might be simpler than he imagined. False optimism was not the shield he wanted, but he was able to tap into a much more real, quiet hope that had been drowned out by his fear.

Courage doesn't always roar. Sometimes courage is the quiet voice at the end of the day saying, "I will try again tomorrow."

—**Mary Anne Radmacher**

Settle yourself and listen for the low, steady voice of hope in you.

I'm a huge Lucille Ball fan. I think she's funnier than just about anyone else I watched on cable TV as a child. As much as her schtick was based on being the ditzy redhead who never did anything right and whose husband roared at her ("Lucy, you got some 'splainin' to do" is the nicest thing I remember him saying to her), I couldn't quite imagine her losing faith in herself.

But, of course, she did, as we all can at some points in our life. I don't think her comedy could be that brilliant if it weren't based on some truth. And she got busy, all right, creating a laughter legacy that's no doubt made millions of us feel more competent and more optimistic.

One of the things I learned the hard way was that it doesn't pay to get discouraged. Keeping busy and making optimism a way of life can restore your faith in yourself.

—**Lucille Ball**

When you feel down and out, keep your hands busy and your spirits light.

Does sharing a good laugh together help us bond with certain people? Or is it because we laugh together that we bond? This is one of those either/or questions to which the answer is yes. Both.

Laugh alone and you won't be for long—laughing alone, that is. Not only is laughter good medicine, it's contagious.

So when the really nasty stuff comes along—the stuff that could turn a person into a pessimistic curmudgeon (say, losing jobs, friends, or lovers, or watching the news on a bad day), then finding the laughter—whether you listen to the jokes or make them—helps in two ways. Laughing lifts the weight a bit, relieves the tension, physiologically and emotionally. And laughter most often attracts laughter, and soon we find ourselves sharing it with our friends and family.

Through humor, you can soften some of the worst blows that life delivers. And once you find laughter, no matter how painful your situation might be, you can survive it.

—**Bill Cosby**

Share the funniest thing you heard today.

W ell, then open the doors and let me in. Havelock Ellis lived in an era when people could say "lunatic asylum" with a straight face. But I wonder if he wasn't speaking tongue-in-cheek? Think of all the wonderful writers, artists, and thinkers who've been holed up in those places in our history.

The loony bin, the day-care center, temples and churches. Where there are children, holy people, madmen, and artists—that's where you'll find optimism. We all have a little of each in us . . . a child who loves ice cream, the depths of our soul where the deepest faith resides, the poet who can turn the simplest observation into a fresh perspective.

The place where optimism most flourishes is the lunatic asylum.

—Havelock Ellis

Find your mad optimist and say what you feel, feel what you know, and let the best that is possible into your heart.

> *Imagination is more important than knowledge. For knowledge is limited to all we now know and understand, while imagination embraces the entire world, and all there ever will be to know and understand.*
>
> **—Albert Einstein**

Dare to imagine today, even if it makes you feel silly.

I am a know-it-all. I have a penchant for memorizing useless information, for adopting (without even realizing it, sometimes) the opinion from the op-ed in the morning paper, for appropriating someone else's smart comments. And then I catch myself, mid-conversation, on autopilot—spewing out knowledge gleaned from the radio, or the paper, or a book, almost word for word. It's embarrassing, frankly.

So why do I do it? Because knowledge is comforting. Feeling smart goes a long way toward feeling safe and good.

But here's the rub. Knowledge, as Einstein says, is limited. Imagination is unlimited. And unlimited is unknown. And unknown can be very scary and doesn't always make for good small talk. Sure, it's important to know things—we couldn't get along without it. But it's more important to delve into the vastness of our imaginations, and to stimulate the imaginations of others. This is the only path to broader knowledge.

There is a vast difference between pessimism and realism. Imagine you live the life of the goldfish, who purportedly doesn't remember from one trip 'round the tank to the next. This may be happiness for the fish, a blissful oblivion, but think of what's comparable in human existence—a vegetative state, or dementia. Hardly bliss. So then you run to the opposite end of the scale—hyperawareness. In our culture we must have a twenty-four-hour live news feed of the latest disaster, and rather than informing us or stimulating us, it depresses and anesthetizes us. We know intuitively that this is not the knowledge and understanding we seek, but it fills our brains just as empty calories fill our stomachs. How can we know more deeply? We can acknowledge and seek to understand the bad in life, the evil in the world, as a means to an end—of change, of understanding, of peace. You cannot combat an evil you refuse to acknowledge—and you cannot grow from a terrified paralysis.

I am not a pessimist; to perceive evil where it exists is, in my opinion, a form of optimism.

—**Roberto Rossellini**

Paralysis is the worst symptom of a pessimistic stance.

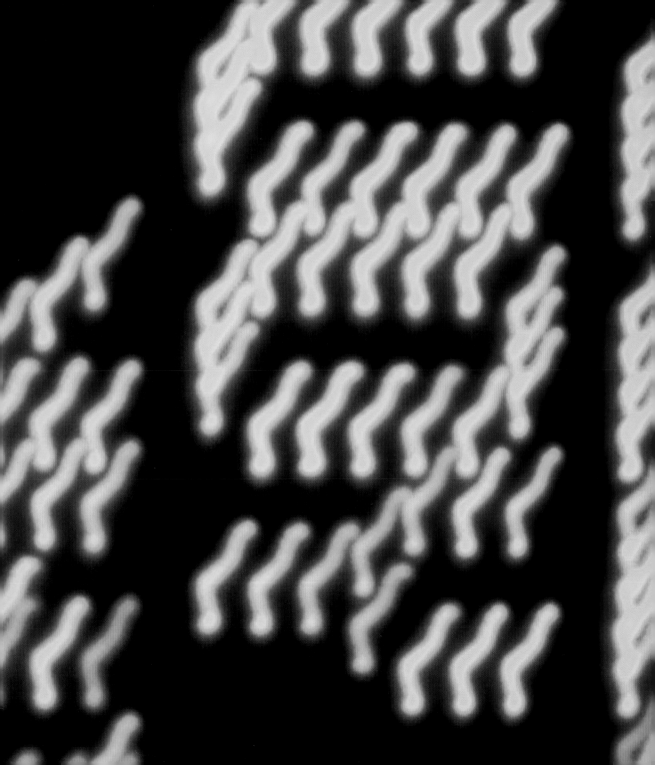

Here's the deal. It doesn't really matter if your glass is actually half full or half empty. At least it doesn't matter to who you essentially are. While what happens to us can influence who we are, ultimately, we choose—yes, choose—how our circumstances affect us.

We are in charge of how we react to our circumstances and what we let our circumstances do to us. This is one of those life lessons that seem counterintuitive. And just when I think I've "got it," it seems I get another chance to practice making a choice under less than ideal circumstances. I'm not less of a person because of circumstances like a colleague being promoted over me. And I get to choose how those circumstances affect me. I can let them wear on me, become bitter, unhappy, maybe get myself fired because of my bad attitude. Or I can look at the whys and hows. I can change my "modus operandi," or maybe I can go out and get a new job because the circumstances of this one don't suit me.

Man is not the creature of circumstances. Circumstances are the creatures of men.

—Benjamin Disraeli

Remind yourself that you're bigger than the sum of your circumstances.

Ask yourself whether you are happy, and you cease to be so.

—John Stuart Mill

Indeed, ask yourself if you are happy and you will stop being anything but *stuck*.

I read the posting of a woman on an anonymous online chat board asking, "How do you know when your marriage is over?" She then listed her husband's upsetting behaviors and detailed her own failed efforts to deal with them. But she was asking the wrong question—one cloaked in fake reason that really not only implied finality and hopelessness but reflected a loss of perspective. Questions are supposed to help us explore a problem, but this one was clearly shutting her down even further.

In an emotional time, a time of frustration, or even when we're just very tired, we sometimes forget how to transform our questions into ones that actually have answers, or that lead to positive actions.

"Am I happy?" is another big trick question—alarm bells should go off whenever anyone asks it. If you are happy, it doesn't occur to you to ask; if you're not, there are more important questions you'd better be asking yourself to change your situation. "Do I have to be happy all the time?" "What little thing can I do today that will make me smile?" "Is there someone else I know who could use cheering up?"

"Am I happy?" is a psychological fake out—a trick we pull on ourselves to feel as if we're making progress, while we firmly plant ourselves in the mud.

I was born in the Midwest, where winter could mean twenty below and the Winnipeg Clipper blowing in hard from the Canadian plains. That was cold. When I was a child, my family moved to California, and my father laughed at people who wore down coats in fifty-two-degree weather. Then I moved to the East Coast. Snow, again, but never twenty below. When I lived in each of those three places, I went with the flow—bundling up like everyone else. Is one person's cold more real than another's? I think not.

What really matters is how you feel about that cold. Twenty below, snow, icy roads—a chance to stay home, cozy around the fire. Or go ice fishing. Fifty-two degrees and raining. Well, it's chilly now, but the hills will be green soon. Wet and windy, forty degrees, but the wisteria will start to bloom in a matter of a few short weeks.

How you look at things matters.

—**From a TV commercial**

See how your perspective can change the weather. (Or at least how you feel about it.)

Turns out you don't need any special materials, or some big chunk of change, to get started on a new positive outlook. That's what's so exciting about it. No installment plan, no mortgage payments, no curbside check-in.

Feeling lucky? Get on the transition train, the magic carpet of curiosity, the steamboat of starting over, the bus of blessings, the surfboard of selflessness, lace up your raucous red roller skates and strap on your wings of wishes and work, and take a road trip to *wheeeeee*!!!!

Optimist: Person who travels on nothing from nowhere to happiness.

—Mark Twain

Drink a great big gulp from your half-full glass of life.

To Our Readers

Conari Press, an imprint of Red Wheel/Weiser, publishes books on topics ranging from spirituality, personal growth, and relationships to women's issues, parenting, and social issues. Our mission is to publish quality books that will make a difference in people's lives—how we feel about ourselves and how we relate to one another. We value integrity, compassion, and receptivity, both in the books we publish and in the way we do business.

Our readers are our most important resource, and we value your input, suggestions, and ideas about what you would like to see published. Please feel free to contact us, to request our latest book catalog, or to be added to our mailing list.

Conari Press
An imprint of Red Wheel/Weiser, LLC
500 Third Street, Suite 230
San Francisco, CA 94107
www.redwheelweiser.com